The Amazing World of Sharks

FRESHWATER
SHARKS

The Amazing World of Sharks

FRESHWATER SHRKS

By Elizabeth Roseborough

MASON CREST

Mason Crest
450 Parkway Drive, Suite D
Broomall, Pennsylvania 19008
(866) MCP-BOOK (toll-free)
www.masoncrest.com

First printing
9 8 7 6 5 4 3 2 1
Printed in the USA

ISBN (hardback) 978-1-4222-4125-7
ISBN (series) 978-1-4222-4121-9
ISBN (ebook) 978-1-4222-7674-7

Library of Congress Cataloging-in-Publication Data

Names: Roseborough, Elizabeth, author.
Title: Freshwater sharks / Elizabeth Roseborough.
Description: Broomall, Pennsylvania: Mason Crest, [2019] | Series: The amazing world of sharks | Includes bibliographical references and index.
Identifiers: LCCN 2018013888 (print) | LCCN 2018018838 (ebook) | ISBN 9781422276747 (eBook) | ISBN 9781422241257 (hardback) | ISBN 9781422241219 (series)
Subjects: LCSH: Sharks--Juvenile literature. | Freshwater fishes--Juvenile literature.
Classification: LCC QL638.9 (ebook) | LCC QL638.9 .R66 2019 (print) | DDC 597.3--dc23
LC record available at https://lccn.loc.gov/2018013888

Developed and Produced by National Highlights Inc.
Editors: Keri De Deo and Mika Jin
Interior and cover design: Priceless Digital Media
Production: Michelle Luke

CONTENTS

KEY ICONS TO LOOK FOR:

Words to Understand: These words with their easy-to-understand definitions will increase the reader's understanding of the text while building vocabulary skills.

Sidebars: This boxed material within the main text allows readers to build knowledge, gain insights, explore possibilities, and broaden their perspectives by weaving together additional information to provide realistic and holistic perspectives.

Educational Videos: Readers can view videos by scanning our QR codes, providing them with additional educational content to supplement the text. Examples include news coverage, moments in history, speeches, iconic sports moments, and much more!

Text-Dependent Questions: These questions send the reader back to the text for more careful attention to the evidence presented there.

Research Projects: Readers are pointed toward areas of further inquiry connected to each chapter. Suggestions are provided for projects that encourage deeper research and analysis.

Series Glossary of Key Terms: This back-of-the book glossary contains terminology used throughout this series. Words found here increase the reader's ability to read and comprehend higher-level books and articles in this field.

FUN FACTS...
GETTING TO KNOW THEM

TIGER SHARK
Named for the vertical striped markings along its body, but they fade with age.

MAKO SHARK
Known as the race car of sharks for its fast swimming speed!

BULL SHARK
Named for its stocky shape, broad, flat snout, and aggressive, unpredictable behavior!

RAYS
Rays and sharks belong to the same family. A ray is basically a flattened shark.

GREAT WHITE SHARK
With jaws this fierce, they don't call it "Great" for nothing!

BLUE SHARK
Known by their distinct blue and white coloring, their large eyes, and long snout.

HAMMERHEAD SHARK
Yes, those are eyes mounted on the side of its head, giving it 360-degree vision!

THRESHER SHARK
This clever shark uses its unique long tail fin to stun and catch prey!

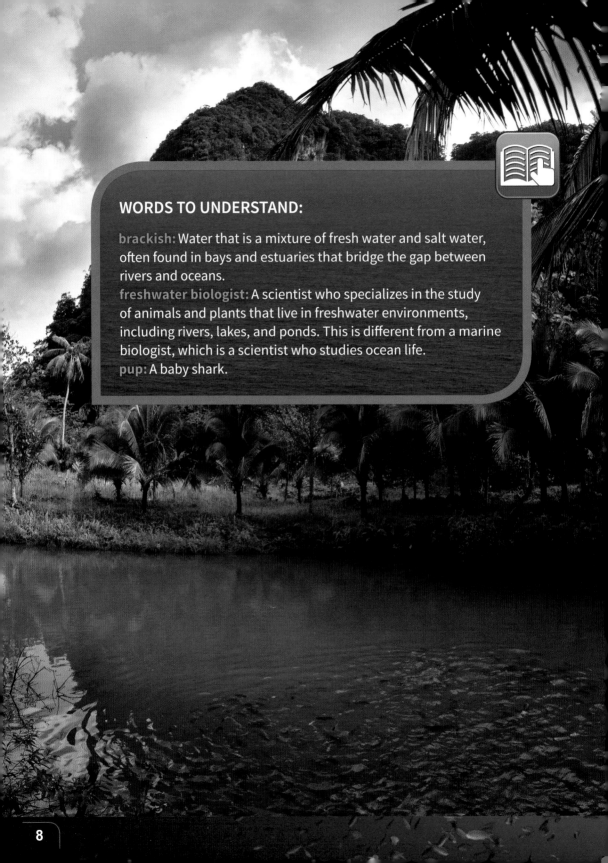

WORDS TO UNDERSTAND:

brackish: Water that is a mixture of fresh water and salt water, often found in bays and estuaries that bridge the gap between rivers and oceans.

freshwater biologist: A scientist who specializes in the study of animals and plants that live in freshwater environments, including rivers, lakes, and ponds. This is different from a marine biologist, which is a scientist who studies ocean life.

pup: A baby shark.

CHAPTER 1

INTRODUCING FRESHWATER SHARKS

When we think about sharks, we usually picture large, scary creatures swimming in the deep blue ocean, with their gray fins poking through the waves. It's easy to imagine that sharks are a danger to humans in the ocean, but most people think that they're safe if they're swimming in a lake or a river. While most sharks are found in salt water, some sharks actually live in fresh water rivers and lakes! Freshwater sharks have adapted to survive without the salt required by ocean-dwelling sharks. Some freshwater sharks live in fresh water only; others are able to go back and forth between fresh and salt water. Some river sharks are known for being sneaky and aggressive—a deadly combination to any human or animal that tries to get in their way. In this book, you'll learn about the different types of freshwater sharks, their habitats and behavior, how they hunt, how they're able to live in fresh water, and what to do if you're in a situation in which you are threatened by a freshwater shark.

Some sharks can be found in rivers and lakes.

Freshwater biologists know of four main types of sharks that spend time in freshwater rivers—the Ganges shark, the northern river shark, the bull shark, and the speartooth shark. We know that there are at least two more types of river sharks, but they are very difficult to locate and study. Freshwater sharks are elusive—they are difficult to spot and tend to keep themselves hidden, swimming near the bottom of deep, murky rivers. Most freshwater sharks are severely endangered; so few of them exist that they are difficult to study. Their tendency to remain out of the sight of humans not only makes it difficult to figure out their behaviors, but also makes it difficult to pin down their exact habitat as well. Freshwater sharks have been spotted in South and Southeast Asia, Africa, North America, New Guinea, and Australia, but it's possible that they exist in other areas of the world as well.

River sharks are hard to find in muddy, dark river water.

Why do young bull sharks enter rivers? Check out this video to learn about why bull sharks choose to leave the ocean and take a swim in fresh water.

Three of the four types of freshwater sharks—the northern river shark, the bull shark, and the speartooth shark—are able to swim in both fresh and salt water. This means that it is especially hard for scientists to track their behaviors, as they are regularly switching between fresh water and salt water. Usually, these sharks spend the majority of their time in salt water, and they swim into freshwater rivers for specific life events, such as giving birth. The Ganges shark is the only shark that must stay in a freshwater environment in order to survive, as it has not adapted to survive in both fresh and salt water. While there are some differences between these four species, there are a few things they have in common. All freshwater sharks have stocky, muscular bodies and tend to be aggressive and unpredictable, especially when provoked. Freshwater sharks tend to have a more fish-like appearance than ocean sharks, making it easy to confuse them with regular river fish. They usually have small eyes and must rely on senses other than their eyesight (such as electroreception) in order to hunt their prey.

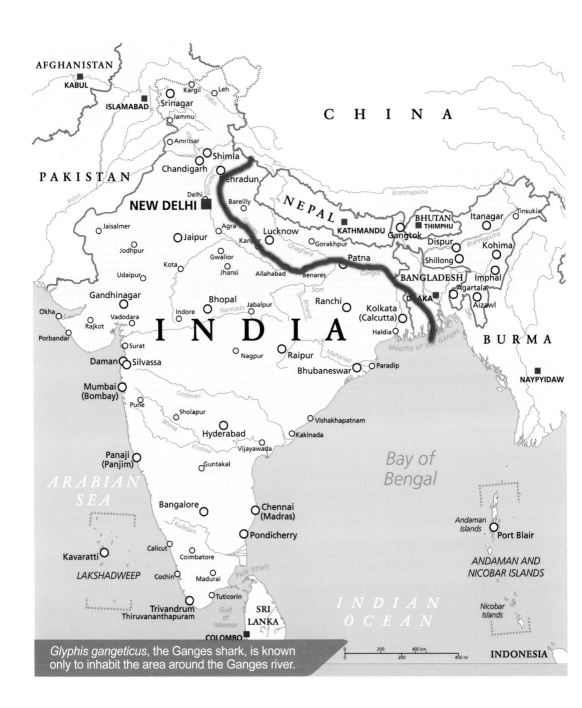

Glyphis gangeticus, the Ganges shark, is known only to inhabit the area around the Ganges river.

HOW DO BIOLOGISTS LEARN ABOUT SHARKS?

Studying sharks can be a dangerous job! Often, biologists track sharks by attaching a receiver to the shark's dorsal (top) fin. This tracker then reports information to either a satellite or a stationary receiver, which then relays information about the shark's movement patterns back to a computer. The computer then generates a map that shows biologists where and how frequently the shark moves. Trackers allow biologists to learn about a shark's habitat, feeding patterns, and mating habits. While tagging sharks does cause a moment of discomfort for the shark, the tag allows scientists to learn valuable information about how to best protect sharks and help increase their populations.

In order to track sharks, biologists have to find them first! With river sharks, this is difficult. Biologists regularly survey, or look over, rivers in search of freshwater sharks, but it's rare that they find them. Sometimes, scientists spend years trying to find certain species, such as the northern river shark. This makes it difficult to fully understand the habitat, diet, and behavior patterns of these sharks. When biologists are unable to study live specimens, they get information from dead sharks that have washed up on beaches and from fossilized sharks that have been preserved for many years. While these methods can provide some information, such as bone structure and habitat, nothing takes the place of being able to study a live shark. Biologists are working every day to come up with more sophisticated shark-locating methods so that they can learn more about these river giants.

GANGES SHARK

Growing to nearly 7 ft. (about 2.13 m) long, the Ganges shark is featured in many stories of sharks attacking (and eating) humans who accidentally venture into its territory. While some people who live in areas frequented by the Ganges shark still believe this to be true, scientists think that this fear is actually a case of mistaken identity, as the Ganges shark is often confused with the more common (and far more aggressive) bull shark. The Ganges shark is only found in the Ganges river of India and Bangladesh. The bull shark is known for swimming in this river as well. Ganges sharks are true river-only sharks and likely are unable to migrate to salt water. Scientists are working to learn more about the Ganges shark, as they are rare, difficult to spot, and pose a possible danger to those working to learn more about them.

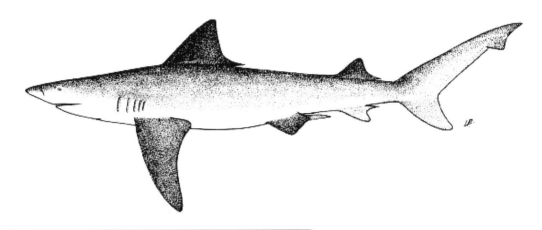

This drawing depicts a Ganges shark. They're so rare, it's difficult to get pictures of them.

SHARK MYTH: SHARKS LIKE TO EAT PEOPLE.

For a shark, eating a person is like humans eating broccoli. Most of us don't care for it, and it's not our first choice. Sharks prefer prey that is meaty and loaded with fat, as they need a high number of calories to support their high activity levels. Most sharks need to swim constantly in order to keep water moving over their gills. When water runs over a shark's gills, this provides them with oxygen, just like breathing provides people with oxygen. This constant need to swim uses a lot of energy. People simply do not have enough fat to meet the caloric needs of a shark. When sharks attack people, it is usually because they feel that their safety, or the safety of their pups, has been threatened. In addition to attacking to protect themselves, many sharks are territorial—they don't like people or animals to be in their personal space, whether they perceive a threat or not.

NORTHERN RIVER SHARK

The northern river shark is found in Australia and New Guinea. These sharks have the ability to thrive in fresh water, brackish water, and salt water. Typically, only young northern river sharks stay in rivers; adults are only seen in

It is rare to find a live northern river shark.

saltwater environments. These sharks tend to prefer extremely turbulent waters, which may explain why, as they grow and gain strength, they begin to prefer rough ocean waters to calm river waters. The force of a strong current allows these sharks to conserve energy, as they do not have to put forth as much effort to swim. Northern river sharks are extremely rare, and much like they are with the Ganges shark, scientists are working hard to locate more of these animals so that they can study them and protect them from harm.

BULL SHARK

Bull sharks are found in shallow coastal waters of Nicaragua, and they are also known for traveling up the Mississippi River in the United States. The vast majority of river shark sightings are bull sharks, as they are far more common than other types of freshwater sharks. While there is not much research on the interactions of freshwater sharks and humans, it's likely that bull sharks are responsible for most reported freshwater shark bites. Bull sharks are known for being aggressive toward both humans and other animals. Bull sharks spend most of their time in salt water, but venture into fresh water to have their babies, which may explain why they are especially territorial in fresh water. Rivers provide a safe place for bull sharks to have their pups, free from the predators they must defend themselves against in the open ocean.

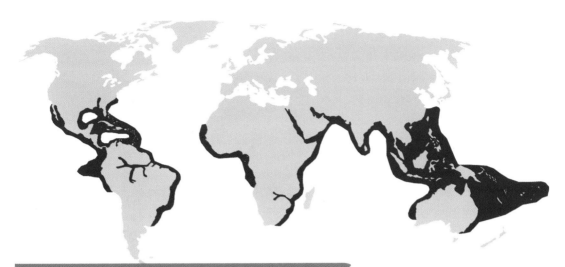

This map shows the suspected distribution of bull sharks, the most well-known species of freshwater shark.

HOW DANGEROUS ARE BULL SHARKS?

In a word: very! All freshwater sharks are known for being difficult to spot, bull sharks included. These predators have a tendency to swim in murky, muddy water, making them nearly invisible to their potential prey. This benefits bull sharks in two ways. First, it makes it easy for them to hunt, as they are able to sneak up on their prey without being seen. Second, it protects them from potential predators. When bull sharks encounter humans, they are often aggressive—even deadly. The bull shark is often referred to as one of the most dangerous sharks to humans, surpassing the great white in terms of aggression and potential to cause harm. Since bull sharks like to hang out in coastal waters, they are likely to encounter humans who are out fishing or enjoying rivers. Bull sharks are territorial, meaning they do not like humans or other animals to enter their space. When a human enters their territory, they are quick to bite. When bull sharks attack, their prey often becomes disoriented because they didn't see the shark coming. Since they often swim close enough to the shore that they share water with humans out for a swim, it's no wonder that bull shark attacks were the inspiration for the novel *Jaws*.

SPEARTOOTH SHARK

The speartooth shark is found in large tropical rivers and coastal marine waters in Australia and New Guinea. There have also been reports of speartooth sharks in the waters of the South China Sea, making it likely that the speartooth shark is capable of traveling long

Speartooth sharks have mostly been found in Australia and New Guinea.

distances in salt water. Like the Ganges shark and the northern river shark, speartooth sharks are extremely rare. Speartooth sharks are able to survive in extremely salty and fresh waters without health issues. They can easily move between the two types of water. However, they are only found in fast-moving, rough waters. Like its cousin, the northern river shark, the speartooth shark prefers these rough currents as the water allows them to conserve valuable energy. Speartooth sharks are excellent hunters, as they have adapted to be able to see their prey even in near-complete darkness. The speartooth shark is not yet well studied, and it's hard to know exactly how many of them live in the wild. Scientists have only been able to observe the speartooth shark in the wild a handful of times, making it difficult to learn about their behavior.

TEXT-DEPENDENT QUESTIONS:

1. What are three traits that all freshwater sharks have in common?

2. Why is it hard for scientists to learn about freshwater sharks?

3. Which type of freshwater shark is most well known for aggressive behavior?

RESEARCH PROJECT:

Ganges sharks are the only freshwater sharks that are not also able to survive in salt water. Research the Ganges shark and find out why they are only able to live in fresh water.

WORDS TO UNDERSTAND:

beached: An animal that is beached has swum onto the shore and become stuck, making them unable to return to the water.

extinct: A species or group that no longer has any living members.

habitat: The natural area in which an animal lives.

sustainable: A sustainable practice is capable of being maintained in a way that does not cause environmental damage.

CHAPTER 2

THE FRESHWATER SHARKS' POPULATION AND HABITAT

Freshwater sharks are found in a variety of locations around the world. Every body of fresh water that connects to the ocean has the potential to hold freshwater sharks, as long as the river is deep enough to support the shark's needs. It's difficult to pin down the exact **habitat** of many freshwater sharks, as they tend to spend much of their time in the ocean and swim into brackish and fresh water when they need to have babies or find food. Many freshwater sharks are also extremely rare, bordering on **extinct**. Scientists do their best to figure out where freshwater sharks live by observing living specimens and fossils when they do not have the ability to observe live sharks.

Freshwater sharks, like this bull shark, tend to swim into rivers to breed or give birth.

HABITAT OF THE GANGES SHARK

The Ganges shark gets its name from its habitat, as it lives in the Ganges River in India. The Ganges River is quite large—it is 1,560 mi. (2,150 km) long and is very wide in most areas. The Ganges River is generally calm and quiet, without turbulent waters. The Ganges River is culturally important to the people of India, as it holds religious significance for Hindus (people who practice Hinduism). Many people use the river for bathing, washing, boating, and swimming. The regular use of this river has led to many stories of the Ganges shark being passed down through generations.

Evidence of Ganges sharks, such as fossils and preserved remains, has also been found in Sri Lanka and Bangladesh. The Ganges shark is the only true freshwater shark in the world, meaning it does not have the capability to survive in salt water. Sadly, the Ganges shark's limited habitat contributes to the fact that its population is declining rapidly. The Ganges River is a hotbed of man-made development and activity, which can negatively impact sharks.

Because of the Ganges shark's elusive nature, it's hard to pinpoint exactly which areas of the Ganges River make up the shark's habitat. Ganges sharks are able to swim with and against the current, allowing it to travel up and down the river. While stories of the Ganges shark are quite popular throughout India, few people have ever seen a Ganges shark in real life.

The Ganges River is an important resource for the Ganges shark and for the people of India.

HABITAT OF THE NORTHERN RIVER SHARK

Also known as the New Guinea river shark, the northern river shark has been observed in the freshwater, brackish water, and salt water areas in and around Australia and New Guinea. The northern river shark is extremely rare, and it's possible that its habitat is actually much larger than the waterways that run through these two countries. Since the northern river shark can survive in salt water just as well as fresh water, it's possible that it could travel through the oceans to the fresh water systems of other countries.

The northern river shark, or New Guinea shark, is found around Australia and New Guinea.

Northern river sharks are so rare that scientists estimate that fewer than 250 of them exist. It's possible that this number could be incorrect—scientists are working hard to continue to study the rivers in the area to see if the northern river shark is more plentiful than they originally thought. Scientists regularly survey rivers that are known for the northern river shark, but it's extremely rare that they actually catch one. These sharks tend to keep themselves hidden when they feel threatened by something that they view as unusual, such as humans.

HABITAT OF THE BULL SHARK

Bull sharks are found in temperate and tropical coastal areas around the world, including the coasts of North America, Asia, South America, Africa, India, and Australia. Bull sharks are known for spending most of their time in salt water. They enter freshwater rivers when it's time for them to have babies. It's unlikely that adult male bull sharks will ever enter a freshwater system. When female bull sharks are in fresh water and about to have pups, they are extremely aggressive toward humans. They prefer to swim in shallow, murky waters, and they do not hesitate to attack any human or animal who enters their territory.

Since bull sharks spend most of their time in salt water, their habitat is typically the open ocean. When it's time for them to have their babies, they enter the nearest freshwater source, meaning they are capable of inhabiting most of the freshwater sources that connect to oceans worldwide. Bull shark sightings and attacks have been reported far into the Mississippi and Ohio Rivers in North America. It's rare for bull sharks to swim hundreds of miles inland, but it has been known to happen. No one is quite sure why bull sharks would swim hundreds of miles away from the ocean, but it's quite possible that they are willing to travel far distances in order to prey upon their favorite foods.

Bull sharks prefer shallow water to deep water. While they are capable of swimming to depths of up to 490 ft. (150 meters), bull sharks prefer not to swim below 98 ft. (30 m). While bull sharks are known for coming close to the shore, any rivers or streams that they enter must be deep enough for them to swim comfortably. It's unusual for a bull shark to swim up an extremely shallow river, as it is possible for them to become beached.

Bull sharks prefer shallow water.

HABITAT OF THE SPEARTOOTH SHARK

Freshwater biologists have observed the speartooth shark in the fast-moving waters of Australia and New Guinea. Much like its cousin, the northern river shark, the speartooth shark is extremely rare. Scientists estimate that there are between 250 and 2,500 speartooth sharks in the wild, but more research needs to be done to fully understand their population and habitat. Speartooth sharks prefer turbulent, fast-moving waters. Instead of constantly swimming, speartooth sharks drift with the current, allowing them to conserve valuable energy. It's likely that speartooth sharks prefer to stay near the surface of the water, allowing them to use the energy of the current as much as possible. While staying near the surface allows speartooth sharks to use sunlight to hunt, this is unnecessary, as this species has evolved to be able to see in near-darkness.

Speartooth sharks prefer fast-moving waters to help them conserve energy.

POPULATION AND CONSERVATION STATUS

Freshwater shark populations are at a dangerous all-time low, and if swift corrective action is not taken, it's likely that freshwater sharks are going to become extinct. There are a number of factors causing freshwater shark populations to decline. Since their numbers are so low, it's difficult for freshwater biologists to know exactly what needs to be done to protect these populations.

NATURAL THREATS TO FRESHWATER SHARKS

The constantly changing environments of many rivers pose natural threats to freshwater shark populations. Seasonal temperature changes, fluctuating oxygen levels, turbidity (roughness of waters), and changing mineral levels can all cause sickness or death to freshwater sharks. Weather patterns, including monsoons and hurricanes, can cause changes to waterways that can negatively impact freshwater sharks. Working to preserve freshwater shark populations can be difficult because scientists are struggling to learn more about these elusive creatures. It's likely that freshwater sharks are able to adapt to a variety of environments, as proven by their ability to survive in fresh water.

MAN-MADE THREATS TO FRESHWATER SHARKS

Commercial and Sport Fishing

While fluctuations in nature make life hard enough for freshwater sharks, there are many human activities that create issues for these populations as well. Freshwater sharks are a common target for sport fishermen (especially the northern river shark, because of the high price some retailers are willing to pay for its jaws). During sport fishing, freshwater sharks are often killed as trophies with little concern for the effect this has on the shark population. In high tourism areas, sport fishing tours are often billed as a once-in-a-lifetime activity. Tourists sign up to go fishing with professional fishermen, ride out into the deep ocean or up the rivers,

This speartooth shark was unlucky enough to be found at the end of a fisherman's pole.

and fish for sharks. It's rare that the tourists actually use the shark for food—more often than not, the dead or dying shark is used as a photo opportunity, and then killed or returned to the ocean in its injured state (most sharks do not survive being out of the water for more than a few minutes). Sometimes, commercial fishermen (people who make money from fishing) catch river sharks and sell their body parts (jaws, teeth) to tourists as souvenirs. The Ganges shark is often hunted for its fins and jaws, and those parts are sold to tourism businesses.

Bycatch

When commercial fishermen go fishing, they often use large nets to catch fish and bring them on board their boats. Usually, they toss the net into the water behind the boat, and then they drive the boat at a high speed, catching fish in the net. While this method is very effective for catching large groups of fish, it's environmentally irresponsible. When a large net is cast into a body of water, it's impossible to determine exactly what animals will be caught in the net. Animals that are unintentionally caught in the net are called bycatch. Sometimes, commercial fishermen simply kill these animals as well. While it may seem like an easy solution to just throw bycatch back into the water, these animals are often tangled and injured by the net. Even when thrown back into the water, it's unlikely that they are able to overcome their net injuries on their own. These animals often die due to infection or starvation (as their injuries keep them from effectively hunting).

Many people are aware of how net fishing can hurt dolphins, but few people are aware that this practice can hurt sharks as well. It's important that net fishing be done in a way that reduces bycatch.

Commercial net fishing can result in bycatch.

Land Development

Land development (construction and building) poses a threat to river sharks. When new buildings are constructed, it's common for area waterways to be disrupted. From dams to bridges, waterway construction can negatively affect the habitat of river sharks. During construction projects, water flow is often changed, slowed, or stopped, which can cause health problems or death for river sharks.

Pollution

When we think of pollution, we often think of litter, floating garbage, and smog in the air. While these things are bad for the environment, water pollution can make it nearly impossible for marine and freshwater animals to live healthy lives. Many factories use water to make their products. Over the course of manufacturing, the water can become contaminated with chemicals. Instead of disposing of this water responsibly, many companies dump the water into rivers. This water can cause a number of negative effects on underwater life. Some of the immediate effects include illness and death. It's also possible for the effects of pollution to last long beyond when the contaminants enter the water. Some chemicals can cause changes in the reproductive organs of underwater animals. This means that when they mate and have babies, the babies are likely to have health issues that will then eventually be passed on to their offspring.

Factories are not the only creators of water pollution. Oil spills are also common creators of pollution. Many companies take oil from under the floor of the ocean, as oil can be sold for a lot of money. This oil sometimes spills into the surrounding ocean, creating health problems and death for ocean animals, including sharks that split their time between fresh water and salt water.

Oil spills cause damage to our oceans and to freshwater fish traveling between fresh water and ocean water.

FRESHWATER SHARKS: CONSERVATION STATUS

There are seven different classification levels to describe the likelihood that plant and animal species will one day cease to exist. From least threat of extinction to most, the levels are data deficient/not evaluated, least concern, conservation dependent, near threatened, vulnerable, endangered, critically endangered, extinct in the wild, and extinct. Currently, the Ganges shark is critically endangered, as is the northern river shark. Since the populations of these two sharks are so low, it's hard for scientists to learn more about them and find out what needs to be done to protect them. Most of the information on these two species comes from studying fossils. While we know the populations of these two species are low, it's also possible that there are more of these sharks than scientists estimate because these sharks tend to spend their time in areas that make it difficult for scientists to observe them. The speartooth shark is listed as endangered. The bull shark is in near-threatened status, making it the freshwater shark with the lowest chance of becoming extinct. It's impossible for scientists to know exactly how many of any type of shark are currently living, so they must do their best to make an estimate of how many are left. They base these numbers on how many of the animal they're able to observe in the wild, either through actual sightings or through tagging. It's especially difficult to figure out how many freshwater sharks are left, as most of them tend to live fairly deep below the surface of the water.

HOW TO HELP

Learning about endangered animals can be sad, and it's easy to feel like there's nothing you can do to make a difference, but nothing could be further from the truth. The only way to make change is for people to step up and take action. There are many things that you can do to help protect freshwater shark populations. One of the most important ways to help protect these animals is simply to raise awareness about why sharks matter. Talking to family and friends about why freshwater sharks are an important part of a river's ecosystem can help change the all-too-common perception that sharks are vicious killers who should be eliminated. Both freshwater and saltwater sharks are an important part of the food chain in their respective environments, and many animals and plants would suffer if sharks ceased to exist. Educating others on why it's not a good idea to buy shark body parts or go on shark-fishing trips can also be an effective way to help keep sharks safe.

To educate your classmates, you can talk to your science teacher and work together to prepare a presentation about why sharks are important. Writing to your local lawmakers about increasing shark protection can also be an effective way to encourage stronger penalties against people who choose to kill or harm sharks. If you do not live in an area with sharks, you can write to lawmakers in the areas in which sharks live and ask them to take action to protect sharks. Before you write, use the internet to look up the laws that currently exist and come up with ideas for how these laws can do an even better job protecting sharks. When you write, make sure you include a return address—many lawmakers are happy to hear from students and would love to write you a letter in return.

When you or your parents purchase seafood (such as tuna), make sure you're purchasing from a company that uses sustainable fishing practices. It's a good idea to look up seafood companies online before making a purchase to find out about how they catch their products. If you find a company that does not practice sustainable fishing, you can write them a letter and tell them that you will not purchase their products until they change their fishing methods.

SIDEBAR

DOING YOUR PART ON VACATION
When you're on vacation, it's important that you do not purchase shark body parts, such as jaws and teeth. While these things may seem like fun souvenirs, they mean that a shark had to die in order to create a product. It's a good idea to stay away from stores that sell these products. It's also important not to eat at restaurants that serve shark fin soup, as many sharks are illegally killed in order to provide the fins for the soup. While it may seem exciting to take a piece of a shark home with you, remember, shark body parts belong on sharks, not in stores.

Watch this video to learn more about how you can do your part to stop sharks from becoming extinct.

Giving to the World Wildlife Fund is one way to help sharks.

In order to help sharks, scientists need to learn more about their habitats, diets, and behavior. Learning more about sharks requires biologists, boats, tagging equipment, travel, shark bait, etc.— all of which can take a lot of time and cost a lot of money. It's a great idea to donate to organizations, such as the World Wildlife Fund, that help us learn more about how to protect endangered and threatened animals. See the internet resources section of this book to learn more about how to give to the WWF.

TEXT-DEPENDENT QUESTIONS:

1. Name two natural threats to freshwater shark populations.

2. The Ganges shark is critically endangered. What does this mean?

3. What two species of freshwater sharks can be found in Australia and New Guinea?

RESEARCH PROJECT:

India recently made a law to protect the Ganges shark. Research the law and explain whether or not you think these regulations will be effective in increasing the Ganges shark population.

WORDS TO UNDERSTAND:

countershading: A type of camouflage exhibited by predators and prey alike in which the upper part of the animal is dark and the underside is light.

osmosis: The movement of molecules through a semi-permeable membrane.

semi-permeable membrane: A layer of a cell (such as those found in shark skin) that allows for certain materials (such as salt water) to pass through.

CHAPTER 3

THE FRESHWATER SHARKS' DIET, BEHAVIOR, AND BIOLOGY

HUNTING & DIET

Ganges Shark

Since the Ganges shark is critically endangered, scientists rarely get a chance to observe one in the wild, as its population numbers are extremely low. This means that scientists have to hypothesize, or make educated guesses, about what the Ganges shark likes to eat. To do this, scientists can use some clues from fossils that have been found. Observing the number, shape, and wear pattern of teeth helps them to understand an animal's diet. It's also helpful to look at the biology of an animal to determine what it eats. Based on its small eyes and slender teeth, it's probable that the Ganges shark is a fish eater. Scientists have also noticed

The Ganges shark is so elusive there are only paintings and drawings available of it.

that the eyes of the Ganges shark are tilted upwards, leading them to hypothesize that the Ganges shark probably swims along the bottom of the river while preparing to attack surface-swimming bony fish. It's likely that Ganges sharks hunt during the day, as they would need the surface of the water to be lit up by the sun because their small eyes are unlikely to allow them to see well in murky river waters. Like many other sharks, the Ganges shark probably stalks its prey from underneath, sprinting upward to make the kill. Since the Ganges shark does not have excellent eyesight, it must depend on other senses in order to hunt including smell, electroreception, and hearing.

Northern River Shark

The northern river shark has a very high number of ampullae of Lorenzini—more than most sharks (all sharks have at least some of these sensory organs). The ampullae of Lorenzini are small pores near the snout that act as electroreceptors, allowing the shark to sense the electrical fields of living things in the area. All living things give out electrical signals, no matter how still they are or how slowly they might be moving. We can't feel these electrical signals, and neither can most other animals. Electricity keeps our hearts pumping and our brains functioning, and the same is true for all members of the animal kingdom. The ampullae of Lorenzini detect the nearby electrical signals and send messages to the shark's brain. The shark's brain interprets these messages and is able to figure out what type of prey is nearby. The shark then decides if it's interested in pursuing the animal. The ampullae of Lorenzini also allow sharks to make a mental map of where prey is hiding, even though they may not be able to see it. Animals put out a different electric frequency when they are injured or distressed, and northern river sharks know that this different frequency signals easy prey. This ability can also help keep sharks safe, as they are able to sense if a large predator is nearby. Like the Ganges shark, the northern river shark's small eyes and slender teeth lead scientists to believe that they are likely to be fish eaters.

The northern river shark has small eyes.

Bull Shark

A formidable predator, the bull shark uses a hunting technique called "bump and bite." The bull shark will headbutt its prey prior to an attack. Since bull sharks do not have very good eyesight, bumping into their prey before attacking gives them a sense of what they are about to eat and whether or not it's going to be worth a fight. Bull sharks are willing to put up a fight while hunting, but they are unlikely to engage in an attack when they are not sure if they will succeed. While bull sharks aren't able to see very well, they do have an excellent sense of smell, and they are able to use that to their advantage when hunting in shallow waters. Like all sharks, bull sharks also use their ampullae of Lorenzini to sense the electrical signals emitted by potential prey.

The bull shark eats different types of food depending on whether it's swimming in fresh water or salt water. In salt water, the bull shark eats dolphins, sea turtles, other sharks, and bony fish—typical of what most saltwater sharks eat. When the bull shark enters fresh water, however, things become more interesting. In fresh water, bull sharks will eat typical underwater fare such as crabs, shrimp, and urchins, but they will also attack land animals, including antelope, hippos, birds, cows, and horses. Of course, bull sharks will only eat land animals if they venture into the water—they are not able to survive and attack on land. Bull sharks are known as opportunistic eaters. This means that when a meal presents itself, bull sharks are not picky—they want to eat!

Bull sharks are not picky eaters. They'll eat whatever they can find, which helps scientists capture them for tagging.

Speartooth Shark

The speartooth shark has small eyes, but scientists believe that they have evolved to have excellent eyesight, being able to see in near-darkness. While scientists are still learning about how speartooth sharks hunt, it's probably true that they depend on their vision, sense of smell, and ampullae of Lorenzini to locate their prey.

Like the Ganges shark and the northern river shark, scientists cannot be completely sure of what the speartooth shark eats, as these animals are so rare that they have not been studied extensively. Fossils and real-life observation have both given a few clues as to their diet. The speartooth shark's small eyes and slim teeth lead scientists to believe that they typically eat fish; however, an adult female speartooth shark was observed with a stingray spine embedded in her jaw. This discovery suggests that speartooth sharks may be adventurous hunters, and their diet may be quite varied.

Scientists know very little about the speartooth shark.

WHAT IS COUNTERSHADING?

Most sharks have a dark upper coloring and a lighter color, ranging from light blue to gray to white, on their bellies. This coloring is known as **countershading**. When viewed from below, the shark's belly allows it to blend in with the sky above, making it nearly invisible to other animals. When viewed from above, the dark coloring allows it to blend in with the dark floor below, allowing it to move around undetected by animals (and humans) on the ocean's surface. Countershading is an important part of hunting for sharks, as well as an important part of staying safe from predators.

BEHAVIOR

Ganges Shark

There is not much that is known about the behavior of the Ganges shark because there are so few of them, and the Ganges sharks that do exist tend to spend much of their time on the murky bottom of the Ganges river, hidden from human view. Many people who live in areas with Ganges sharks have the fear that these sharks regularly attack humans. Scientists are pretty sure this is not the case, as they are constantly looking for Ganges sharks so that they can continue to research them, and they are nearly impossible to find. Much of the common knowledge about the Ganges shark is based on legends, not on actual fact. While these legends may have some truth to them, scientists need to find evidence before they can believe these stories (such as those about the violent nature of the Ganges shark) to be true. It's likely that the Ganges shark spends most of its time on the bottom of the Ganges River, rising to the surface only when it needs to do so to hunt. It's possible that the Ganges shark migrates up and down the Ganges River, but again, more research needs to be done to confirm this behavior. Freshwater biologists have confirmed that the Ganges shark does not migrate in order to mate or have babies, so it's unclear what benefit migration might provide this species.

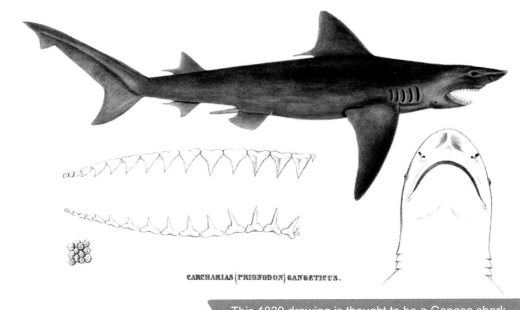

CARCHARIAS (PRIONODON) GANGETICUS.

This 1839 drawing is thought to be a Ganges shark, and it shows great detail of its biology.

Northern River Shark

Scientists are working hard to learn more about the behavior of the northern river shark. We know that northern river sharks enjoy turbulent waters, but it's unclear whether or not this is related to their hunting and mating behavior. Turbulent waters make it easier for them to swim, but there may be additional benefits to preferring this type of environment. Northern river sharks are not aggressive, and there has never been a report of an attack on humans. It's likely that these sharks are shy when it comes to humans and predators, and choose to swim away when they see a potential threat. Their extremely high number of ampullae of Lorenzini makes it unlikely that they need to put a lot of physical effort into hunting, as their electroreception does much of the work for them.

Bull Shark

Known for their aggressive and unpredictable nature, bull sharks are some of the most formidable predators known to man. There have been seventy-seven recorded bull shark attacks on humans, some of them unprovoked.

While bull sharks often swim in salt water, they are equally able to survive in fresh water, and they migrate to rivers and lakes to have babies. Bull sharks have been seen swimming against the current in rivers, working hard to reach freshwater lakes. They are extremely strong swimmers.

The bull shark is fairly social, and is often seen hunting in groups with other bull sharks. It seems that the larger females are dominant over the males.

Bull sharks are often observed waiting at the mouth of the river for fish to swim into their mouths.

Speartooth Shark

Speartooth sharks seem to be quite sluggish, usually choosing to move with the tide instead of swimming against it. This allows them to conserve energy, which helps them to survive during periods in which food is scarce. Speartooth sharks do not seem to show a general preference for day or night, likely because their eyes are not very effective at picking up light. They may even be unable to distinguish daytime from nighttime.

BIOLOGY

In order to understand how freshwater sharks survive, it's important to first understand the biology of saltwater sharks. Most sharks need salt water in order to survive. Sharks do not have to drink ocean water in order to get salt into their bodies, however. Of course, they naturally drink some water when they hunt and eat, but this is not necessary for their health. They are able to absorb salt water (or fresh water) through their skin. To understand why most sharks need salt water, it's necessary to understand the concept of osmosis. Osmosis is when a fluid, such as salt water, moves back and forth through a semi-permeable membrane, such as the skin of a shark. The salt water continues to move back and forth until the concentration of salt is the same inside the membrane (inside the shark's body) as it is outside the membrane (in the ocean water). Since most sharks have evolved and live in salt water, they tend to have very salty bodies, matching the salt level of the ocean around them. When the salt level of the water around the shark changes, many sharks are unable to adapt and thrive because this also changes the level of salt inside their bodies.

Why don't freshwater sharks need to drink water? Watch this video to learn more.

This might lead you to believe that freshwater sharks do not have salty bodies, but interestingly, the opposite is true. Their bodies tend to have twice the amount of salt as the bodies of the animals around them. Due to osmosis, you might think that this would mean the body of the shark would swell, because it is constantly being infused with fresh water in an attempt to make the amount of salt inside the shark's body equal to the amount of salt in the freshwater environment.

Freshwater sharks, however, have a solution to this problem—they urinate very, very frequently, allowing them to get rid of the water that constantly flows through their skin. Freshwater sharks urinate at twenty times the rate of saltwater sharks. This means a few things for their bodies. First, their kidneys must work incredibly hard to process that amount of urine out of their bodies. While this stresses the kidneys, it also requires their bodies to provide a lot of extra energy. While this sounds difficult, freshwater sharks have adapted to process this extra water quite efficiently. Sharks that swim in both salt water and fresh water are able to adjust their bodies based on what type of water they are in.

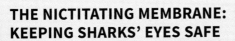

SIDEBAR

THE NICTITATING MEMBRANE: KEEPING SHARKS' EYES SAFE

Some sharks, such as Ganges sharks, have a third eyelid that protects their eyes in dangerous situations, such as during altercations with other animals or while hunting. This organ is called the nictitating membrane. The nictitating membrane is a thin, translucent piece of tissue that protrudes from the inner corner of the eye. When a shark is approaching prey, or is being attacked by another animal, the nictitating membrane emerges from the inner corner of the eye and spreads itself over the shark's eyeball, protecting its vision in case a fight occurs. If the eye is attacked, the nictitating membrane will become injured instead of the shark's eyeball. Most animals that have a nictitating membrane are capable of completely hiding it during normal activity. If you have a cat or a dog at home, it's easy to see the nictitating membrane when he or she is waking up from a nap—it's usually still able to be seen in the inner corner of the eyes. Sharks depend on their eyesight both for catching prey and for keeping themselves safe from predators, so it's important that their eyes are protected.

BIOLOGY OF THE GANGES SHARK

Size

The Ganges shark is quite small at birth, measuring approximately 2 ft. long (0.5 m). At full maturity, its size ranges from 6 to 7 ft. (1.8 to 2 m) long.

Physical Appearance

Like all freshwater sharks, Ganges sharks are stocky and muscular. They have two dorsal (top) fins, and the second one is half the size of the first. Ganges sharks range in color from gray to brown, without any stripes or markings. Their noses (snouts) are broad and round, and their mouths are very long—they extend back towards their eyes. The Ganges shark's eyes are very small and they are tilted upwards. An upward eye tilt is rare among sharks, and it provides a specific advantage. This tilt allows Ganges sharks to swim along the bottom of the river and scan the waters close to the surface

There is some dispute as to whether or not this 1878 drawing is actually a Ganges shark.

for prey. Their upper teeth are high, broad, serrated, and triangular. Their lower teeth are smaller, and they curve inward like claws, making it easier to catch prey. Ganges sharks typically have between thirty-two and thirty-seven rows of teeth in their upper jaws and thirty-one to thirty-four rows of teeth in their lower jaws.

BIOLOGY OF THE NORTHERN RIVER SHARK

Size

The northern river shark is one of the rarest sharks in the world, making it hard to know exactly how large they can become. Since the species was discovered in 1986, only thirty-six of these sharks have ever actually been observed in the wild. So far, northern river sharks have been known to grow up to 9.8 ft. (3 m) long.

Physical Appearance

Northern river sharks have a dark gray top and a light gray or white belly. Their eyes are small, and it's not likely that they use their eyesight as a prime hunting tool. They have a muscular body, a high back, a wide and flat head, and a broad, round snout. Their nostrils are covered with a small, triangular flap of skin. In the upper jaw, northern river sharks have thirty-one to thirty-four rows of teeth. In the lower jaw, they have thirty to thirty-five rows of teeth. Their upper teeth are triangular and serrated (like the edge of a steak knife).

BIOLOGY OF THE BULL SHARK

Size

Bull sharks are quite large, and females are larger than males. At birth, bull sharks are up to 2.7 ft. (0.8 m) long. On average, adult female bull sharks are 7.9 ft. (2.4 m) long and weigh 290 lb. (130 kg). Adult male bull sharks are slightly smaller on average, with a length of 7.4 ft. (2.25 m) and a weight of 209 lb. (95 kg). Much larger bull sharks have been reported—there is one bull shark on record that weighed 694 lbs. (about 314.79 kg)! It's possible that bull sharks even larger than this could exist.

Physical Appearance

The dorsal side of bull sharks is light to dark gray, eventually fading to a white belly. Bull sharks are wider and heavier than most sharks (even heavier than other freshwater sharks). Bull sharks can have up to fifty rows of teeth, with seven teeth in each row.

Bull sharks tend to be wider and heavier than most sharks.

BIOLOGY OF THE SPEARTOOTH SHARK

Size

At birth, speartooth sharks are approximately 2 ft. (0.6 m) long. The largest speartooth shark on record was 5.8 ft. (1.8 m) long, but scientists estimate that speartooth sharks can grow between 6.6 and 9.9 ft. (2 to 3 m) in length.

Physical Appearance

Closely related to the northern river shark, the speartooth shark also has a dark gray top and a light gray or white belly, as well as small eyes that are likely not much use for hunting.

Speartooth sharks are related to the northern river shark and are similar in color and size.

TEXT-DEPENDENT QUESTIONS:

1. The Ganges shark's eyes are tilted upwards. How does this help it hunt?

2. How does countershading keep sharks safe?

3. How many northern river sharks have been observed in the wild?

RESEARCH PROJECT:

Sharks have tons of teeth! Research the different types of shark teeth, and find out which species of shark has the most teeth.

WORDS TO UNDERSTAND:

captivity: A man-made animal habitat, such as an aquarium or zoo.

estuary: The area in which a large river meets the ocean.

self-preservation: A basic instinct in most humans and animals to protect oneself from harm or death.

CHAPTER 4

ENCOUNTERING FRESHWATER SHARKS

SHARK ATTACK!

While most sharks will attack if they feel provoked or threatened, the bull shark is famous for attacking people in both fresh and salt water. Many scientists believe that the bull shark is one of the most dangerous sharks in the world, ranked at the same level as great whites and tiger sharks. Ganges sharks, northern river sharks, and speartooth sharks are not known for coming into contact with or harming humans.

Although bull sharks are dangerous, they won't attack if they feel safe.

An estuary is where a river meets the ocean. This is the Swartkops River mouth and estuary in South Africa.

Since bull sharks are known for preferring shallow waters and **estuaries** near the coastline (whether they're in fresh or salt water), they naturally come into contact with humans more often than other sharks do. Their territorial nature means that they will not hesitate to attack when they feel threatened by a human, animal, or other shark. While bull sharks do not prefer to eat humans, attacks often happen in murky water, as the shark takes a bite out of **self-preservation** or curiosity. It's important to stay out of murky, shallow waters in areas known for having a high number of bull sharks.

WHAT SHOULD YOU DO IF YOU SEE A SHARK?

Imagine it: you're on vacation with your family, swimming or floating in an exotic river, when you see a rubbery gray fin poking up out of the water. What should you do?

First, there are a few things to consider before you find yourself in this situation. It's a good idea to stay out of waters that are known for having high levels of shark activity. It's also important to stay out of murky, muddy waters in which it's difficult to see what is swimming next to you. Timing matters too—sharks are most likely to look for prey in the early morning and early evening hours. When you're in the water, it's a good idea to dress in muted colors, as sharks are attracted to high contrast clothing, such as bright orange and yellow. It's also a good idea to keep an eye on the other animals in the area. If turtles and frogs suddenly make a run for it, it's likely that a threat is approaching.

If a shark is sighted, exit the water quickly and quietly. Even a small shark can cause a lot of damage, so it's important that you leave as fast as possible, no matter how interested you might be in the shark. If you feel something brush against your skin, check to make sure that you have not been bitten, as many shark-bite victims report that they feel no pain. If a shark approaches you and you are unable to exit the water (because you are diving or snorkeling perhaps), stay as still as possible as the shark approaches, and then swim away quickly and quietly.

If a shark attacks you, avoid hitting it with your bare hands if at all possible. Use any hard object you have at your disposal (such as a camera) to hit the shark instead, as this is likely to cause the shark to see you as more of a threat, making it more likely that the shark will swim away. You'll want to hit the shark in the eyes, gills, and snout, as these areas are most sensitive and a hit in these areas is likely to make the shark realize that you are not worth its trouble. If a shark manages to get you in its mouth, fight as aggressively as possible. Playing dead does not work. Continue to try to claw at the shark's gills and eyes. If you are bitten, exit the water quickly and quietly. While it's unlikely that a shark would attack you for a second time, it does happen. When you are out of the water, seek the attention of a medical professional, even if the bite is small.

Remember—while it's good to know what to do in case of a shark attack, it's very unlikely that this will ever happen to you. Shark attacks are extremely rare, and the fear of shark attacks should not stop you from swimming outdoors.

Shark attacks are rare, but it's good to be prepared.

OBSERVING FRESHWATER SHARKS

Unlike saltwater sharks, it is difficult to observe most freshwater sharks in the wild because most of them do not come near the surface of the water and they are very difficult to find. It is possible to observe bull sharks in the ocean, but it is not a good idea to get near them in fresh water as they only venture into fresh water to have their babies. Most animals are more likely to become aggressive when they are protecting their young.

Bull sharks hang out in shallow water the most.

THE GANGES SHARK: A MAN EATER?

In Asia, the Ganges shark is often referred to as a man-eater; however, it's not likely that this is actually true. There are so few Ganges sharks that it's unlikely that the vast majority of people will ever even see one in the wild. While shark attacks do happen in the Ganges River, it's much more likely that bull sharks are actually responsible for the attacks. Bull sharks and Ganges sharks look similar to one another and are found in the same waters. The Ganges shark's teeth are not fit to attack large animals (as they are quite small). However, the bull shark's teeth are perfectly suited for attacking very large prey.

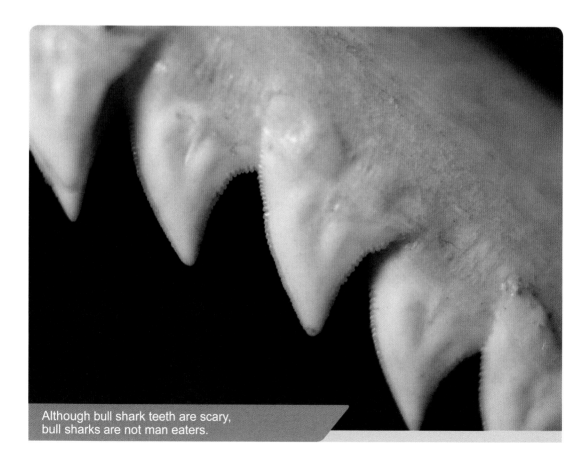

Although bull shark teeth are scary, bull sharks are not man eaters.

Watch this story about bull sharks attacking people swimming in a river in India.

FRESHWATER SHARKS IN CAPTIVITY

Like most saltwater sharks, freshwater sharks tend to not do well in captivity (such as in an aquarium). Most sharks need to move constantly to keep water flowing over their gills, and this is difficult for sharks to do when aquarium walls confine them.

The Lisbon Oceanarium is one of the very few aquariums to keep sharks.

Stay alert, but don't let a fear of sharks keep you from enjoying the water.

TEXT-DEPENDENT QUESTIONS:

1. What are two things you should do to avoid getting attacked by a shark?

2. Why do most scientists believe that bull sharks are actually responsible for shark attacks in the Ganges River?

3. Why can't aquariums keep most sharks in captivity?

RESEARCH PROJECT:

Research news articles about shark attacks and learn more about recent river shark attacks, including where they happen and what type of sharks are involved.

SERIES GLOSSARY OF KEY TERMS

Apparatus: A device or a collection of tools that are used for a specific purpose. A diving apparatus helps you breathe under water.

Barbaric: Something that is considered unrefined or uncivilized. The idea of killing sharks just for their fins can be seen as barbaric.

Buoyant: Having the ability to float. Not all sharks are buoyant. They need to swim to stay afloat.

Camouflage: To conceal or hide something. Sharks' coloring often helps camouflage them from their prey.

Chum: A collection of fish guts and fish remains thrown into the ocean to attract sharks. Divers will often use chum to help attract sharks.

Conservation: The act of preserving or keeping things safe. Conservation is important in keeping sharks and oceans safe from humans.

Decline: To slope down or to decrease in number. Shark populations are on the decline due to human activity.

Delicacy: Something, particularly something to eat, that is very special and rare. Shark fin soup is seen as a delicacy in some Asian countries, but it causes a decline in shark populations.

Expedition: A type of adventure that involves travel for a specific purpose. Traveling to a location specifically to see sharks would be considered an expedition.

Ferocious: Describes something that is mean, fierce, or extreme. Sharks often look ferocious because of their teeth and the way they attack their prey.

Finning: The act of cutting off the top (dorsal) fin of a shark specifically to sell for meat. Sharks cannot swim without all of their fins, so finning leads to a shark's death.

Frequent: To go somewhere often. Sharks tend to frequent places where there are lots of fish.

Ft.: An abbreviation for feet or foot, which is a unit of measurement. It is equal to 12 inches or about .3 meters.

Indigenous: Native to a place or region.

Intimidate: To scare or cause fear. Sharks can intimidate other fish and humans because of their fierce teeth.

Invincible: Unable to be beaten or killed. Sharks seem to be invincible, but some species are endangered.

KPH: An abbreviation for kilometers per hour, which is a metric unit of measurement for speed. One kilometer is equal to approximately .62 miles.

M: An abbreviation for meters, which is a metric unit of measurement for distance. One meter is equal to approximately 3.28 feet.

Mi.: An abbreviation for miles, which is a unit of measurement for distance. One mile is equal to approximately 1.61 kilometers.

Migrate: To move from one place to another. Sharks often migrate from cool to warm water for several different reasons.

MPH: An abbreviation for miles per hour, which is a unit of measurement for speed. One mile is equal to approximately 1.61 kilometers.

Phenomenon: Something that is unusual or amazing. Seeing sharks in the wild can be quite a phenomenon.

Prey: Animals that are hunted for food—either by humans or other animals. It can also mean the act of hunting.

Reputable: Something that is considered to be good or to have a good reputation. When diving with sharks, it is important to find a reputable company that has been in business for a long time.

Staple: Something that is important in a diet. Vegetables are staples in our diet, and fish is a staple in sharks' diets.

Strategy: A plan or method for achieving a goal. Different shark species have different hunting strategies.

Temperate: Something that is not too extreme such as water temperature. Temperate waters are not too cold or too hot.

Tentacles: Long arms on an animal that are used to move or sense objects. Octopi have tentacles that help them catch food.

Vulnerable: Something that is easily attacked. We don't think of sharks as being vulnerable, but they are when they're being hunted by humans.

INDEX

FURTHER READING

Dawson, Scott & Lauren Tarshis. *I Survived: The Shark Attacks of 1916.* New York: Scholastic Publishing, 2010.

DK Publishing. *Everything You Need to Know About Sharks.* New York: DK Publishing, 2012.

Harvey, Derek. *Super Shark Encyclopedia and Other Creatures of the Deep.* New York: DK Publishing, 2015.

Miles Kelly Publishing. *100 Things You Should Know About Sharks.* New York: Barnes and Noble, 2005.

Musgrave, Ruth. *Everything Sharks.* Washington: National Geographic Society, 2011.

INTERNET RESOURCES

http://cnso.nova.edu: The Halmos College of Natural Sciences and Oceanography provides shark videos and shark activity maps.

http://cnso.nova.edu/sharktracking: The Guy Harvey Research Institute (GHRI) Shark Tracking partners with the Halmos College of Natural Sciences and Oceanography in tracking and recording shark activity. The GHRI dedicates its resources to the preservation of marine life, including sharks.

https://www.discovery.com/tv-shows/shark-week/: Check out the Discovery Channel's shark week website for informative videos, quick facts, and photos of sharks of all kinds.

http://saveourseas.com: The Save Our Seas Foundation focuses their efforts specifically on saving sharks and rays. Their website includes shark facts, a newsletter, and details about how to help save sharks and rays.

https://www.sharksider.com/sharks-live-freshwater/: On the Shark Sider site, you'll find information on a variety of species of sharks.

https://www.worldwildlife.org: The World Wildlife Fund is a virtual encyclopedia of information, photos, and stories about endangered and threatened animals. On this site, you can learn about animals, make donations to help animals, and find out more about how to help save endangered species.

AT A GLANCE

Hammerhead Sharks
Length: 20 ft. (6.1 m)
Swim Depth: 262 ft. (80 m)
Lifespan: 20+ years

Bull Sharks
Length: 11.1 ft. (3.4 m)
Swim Depth: 492 ft. (150 m)
Lifespan: 18+ years

Rays
Length: 8.2 ft. (2.5 m)
Swim Depth: 656 ft. (200 m)
Lifespan: 30 years

Great White Sharks
Length: 19.6 ft. (6 m)
Swim Depth: 820 ft. (250 m)
Lifespan: 30 years

Blue Sharks
Length: 12.5 ft. (3.8 m)
Swim Depth: 1,148 ft. (350 m)
Lifespan: 20 years

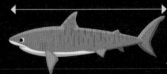

Tiger Sharks
Length: 11.5 ft. (3.5 m)
Swim Depth: 1148 ft. (350 m)
Lifespan: 50 years

Thresher Sharks
Length: 18.7 ft. (5.7 m)
Swim Depth: 1200 ft. (366 m)
Lifespan: 50 years

Mako Sharks
Length: 13.1 ft. (4 m)
Swim Depth: 1,640 ft. (500 m)
Lifespan: 32 years

SWIM DEPTH

200 ft.
400 ft.
600 ft.
800 ft.
1,000 ft.
1,200 ft.
1,400 ft.
1,600 ft.
1,800 ft.

Source: www.iucnredlist.org

PHOTO CREDITS

EDUCATIONAL VIDEO LINKS

Chapter 1
Check out this video to learn about why bull sharks choose to leave the ocean and take a swim in fresh water: http://x-qr.net/1Du7

Chapter 2
Watch this video to learn more about how you can do your part to stop sharks from becoming extinct: http://x-qr.net/1FrK

Chapter 3
Why don't freshwater sharks need to drink water? Watch this video to learn more: http://x-qr.net/1Ewf

Chapter 4
Watch this story about bull sharks attacking people swimming in a river in India: http://x-qr.net/1FsY

AUTHOR'S BIOGRAPHY

Elizabeth Roseborough is a former college, high school, and middle school biology instructor. When not visiting her favorite Caribbean islands, Elizabeth spends her time with her husband, son, and their fur babies, Titan and Stella, at their home in Dayton, Ohio.